[COME CLEAN]

WISCONSIN POETRY SERIES

Edited by Ronald Wallace and Sean Bishop

COME CLEAN

JOSHUA NGUYEN

The University of Wisconsin Press

Publication of this book has been made possible, in part, through support from the Brittingham Trust.

The University of Wisconsin Press
728 State Street, Suite 443
Madison, Wisconsin 53706
uwpress.wisc.edu

Gray's Inn House, 127 Clerkenwell Road
London EC1R 5DB, United Kingdom
eurospanbookstore.com

Printed in the United States of America
This book may be available in a digital edition.

Library of Congress Cataloging-in-Publication Data
Names: Nguyen, Joshua, author.
Title: Come clean / Joshua Nguyen.
Other titles: Wisconsin poetry series.
Description: Madison, Wisconsin : The University of Wisconsin Press, [2021] | Series: Wisconsin poetry series
Identifiers: LCCN 2021013954 | ISBN 9780299336042 (paperback)
Subjects: LCGFT: Poetry.
Classification: LCC PS3614.G885 C66 2021 | DDC 811/.6—dc23
LC record available at https://lccn.loc.gov/2021013954

for my family

SAVE ME, MARIE KONDO

When you put your house in order, you put your affairs and your past in order, too

I open
    my jaw to a framed photo

        of a grandmother I know
        from my first memory:

[hospital bed]

        it picks, picks & scoops
        little droplets of honey

            with a toothpick made from splinters

[half-used tiger balm]

            in the door. Her shoulder smells
            of incense, lavender, love.

                Everyone around me—cousins, uncles,
                        third cousins, friends of cousins—

[ekg machine]

                is crying. My father cries a sound
                        I will never hear again. His mouth lock

                    jawed over the beige mound
                        at the foot of the bed. Ten
                            lifeless toes

[rosary]

crease beneath the hospital blanket.

[[or]]

I open
my jaw to a grandmother
from my first memory—

it splinters
like ice in Texas.

Her shower smells
of incense & Wisconsin [& never crying again].

Everyone around me—cousins, uncles
& the one [ ] who grabbed me—
cries. I'm crying, but a father
will never come near again. My childhood room locked,
reading bedtime stories
that shovel the attic [within the attic]
[ ], [ ], open.

[this box for the herbs]
[this box for the knives]
[this box for all her áo dài]
[this box for her đồng]
[this box for her pearls]
[this box for her globes]
[this box for her purple robes]
[this box for the cognac]
[this box for the hail marys]
[this box for the rice paper]
[this box for the orange star]
[this box for the tar]

[[or]]

Memory [is a grandmother's jaw]:

it splinters.

CONTENTS

[]

I am relieved that I'd left my room tidy,

they'll think of me kindly,

when they come for my things.

MITSKI

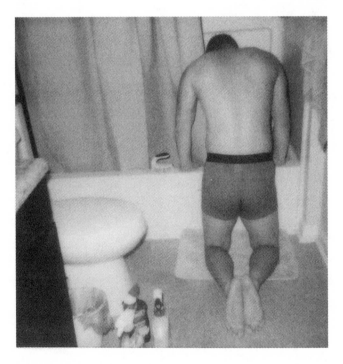

MARCH 4TH

Tell the priest to wait outside the hospital room,

I am wiping the blood off his handsome head.

My son must be presentable to the world.

    My son, the world will try to bury you.

    Your name will be Trung: meaning loyalty or a made bed every morning.

    I sent your father home to tidy up the house.

    I hid a bottle of fish sauce in your crib.

        Do not ever forget that I am your mother.

        I will give you a clean life.

        I will stitch you a towel out of lullabies.

        I will hold you in one hand & a napkin in the other.

            You will collect the dust from the attic, catch it on your tongue.

            You will be porcelain, jade & the slipping of dishes into the sink.

            You will be hair slicked back, skin clear & mouth compressed.

But right now, this moment, you are gunk, you are imperfect.

You are a dragonfly made of placenta rouge.

Right now, I have your blood & my blood cradled.

A sacred intimacy: seeing your filthy innocence.

MY FIRST MEMORY

was four-year-old me drooling over my mother's bare shoulder.
She makes sure to keep swaying because she needs me to stay quiet,
to not interrupt the drowning at the foot of the hospital bed,
where my father lays sprawled, his legs floating on the linoleum.
His hands tuck in his mother's left foot, holding onto her last exhale.

The doctor says something where his mouth contorts into a garrote.
My father lets out a cry: a hook that tears itself into my earlobe:
the kind of childlike wail that disrupts the homily until the echo
is carried away outside & you know they feel awful & it's not their fault
but after you drag your finger through the water & see them red
& exasperated outside, you say nothing to them.

What is the worth of pride when your boat burns into the ocean?
When you are the fire & the ship sinking & the salt digging into eyes?
Skin of your hands torn from holding the anchor dragged by the riptide.
What, then, can a circling family in the hospital do when the captain
is damning the god his mother reminded him to pray to every night
because she said *how do you know when it will be your time?*
Even though, a week prior, my parents were asking around for white
headbands, incense & life vests to prepare for the funeral.

WISCONSIN HAS A PLACE IN MY HEART
& I JUST WANT IT TO LET GO

Thomas tells me that trauma is trite.
That to open up wounds is to bleed yourself out.
Snow, in Wisconsin, blocks the front door of my cousin's house.

In the north, the foyer has stairs up & down.
The basement, in broad daylight, is a gray sky. A groaning
fly by my ear: the only other noise besides

the flinching of my arms.
My cousin's breath,
heavy on my neck.

[ ]

Heavy on my neck:
my cousin's breath,
the flinching of arms,

a fly by my ear. The only other noise beside
the basement, in broad daylight, is the sky groaning gray.
In the north, the foyer has stairs covered up & down

in snow. Wisconsin blocks the front door of my cousin's house.
It opens up wounds. *Bleed yourself out,*
Thomas tells me. Trauma is trite.

MY MARIE KONDO MANIFESTO

There is an order for the way you order: clothes, books, papers, komono. Kiss your items one last time: bedding for the guest that never comes, empty bottles of cognac on the shelf & all the postcards from Mississippi. *Does it spark joy?* Clothes, books, papers, komono. Store everything away. Things barely used will shift towards the back. The back of the drawer filled with fancy socks. Light that never reaches underneath the bed. Clothes, books, papers, komono. Shoeboxes as little homes. Shoebox lids as shelf liners. Catch the spices as they fall. Clothes, books, papers, komono. Take everything out of their crevices: memories you can't forget, photos that develop with red eye & unbleachable clothes. Books by authors that will become monsters. Papers ripped from the diary. The rest of the komono stacked above the cabinets. Embrace the dying of the dust. Conquering eternal entropy. Fabric feathered with the past. Spines misshapen from labor. Documents that tell you to go back home. Clutter reaching the corners of your ceiling. Tidying is to confront yourself. Live for this. For this unpacking. For this organization. The neatly packaged jade bracelet. The white bins in the cupboard. The thirteen trash bags at the end of the driveway. A breathable space to sprawl. Sweat from the tidying. Legs & arms quartered by the corners of the room. See the room clearly. The walls peeling your whole life. Beneath the primer— more wall.

FATHER, THE FATHER

A respiratory therapist walks
into a fever-check, into
a hospital.

My father finds a thermometer
inside a used mask buried
under the Red Lobster.

My family lights a candle
for protection, when uncertainty
comes as a hurricane.

An education will wring
me from the sponge
it came from.

A discotheque plays
tango & my mother
& father fever the groove out.

AMERICAN LỤC BÁT FOR WASHING RICE

Pour water
over the rice & shower
the husk until you get murky
liquid. Clean thoroughly
by turning wrists quick in small
circular motions. All
the milk-water will fall into
the sink. Be careful. You
best not drop one too many
grains—a waste. Family
meals don't come easy. Save all
that you can. Don't withdraw
from the table if all your food
isn't in you or would
you rather kneel on hardwood on rice?
Fifteen belt whips on ice?
Then you learn to make rice. I am
your *mẹ*. I love you *em.*
Now, do as I say: empty the pot
& try again with all your gut.

MY BROTHER EXPLAINS DRIVING

You are eight & I am twenty-five.

You are eight & you will watch me leave.

You are eight & I will follow the mailman across the sea.

You are eight & you will learn the price of stamps at the post office.

You are eight & I will forge two homes from rice paddies.

You are eight & you will steal eggs from your sister's bowl.

You are eight & I will fall in love.

You are eight & you will fall in love.

You are eight & I know nothing.

You are eight & you understand everything.

You are eight & I will be ready to drown when I cross the bridge.

You will watch the flapping.

A DIRTY FLOOR IN THE KEY OF ELBOWS

After Jericho Brown

There is dust on the floor of my cousin's basement.
I know this because my face has been close—
close enough to hear the core of maggots.

If you're close enough to hear the core of maggots,
it's time to clean the floor. A bucket of water
still hits the tile even after dousing it over your head.

I hit the tile after you douse my head.
My parents, upstairs, talking about Vietnamese politics
& which niece will be the most successful, won't appear.

Which knees will be the most successful?
My own? Bent, helping me roll onto my sides.
Yours? A thumbtack pinning me to the ground.

Like a thumbtack pinned to the ground,
I arch my back towards an ambivalent god. I scrub
with the centripetal beauty of my elbow.

The centripetal beauty of elbows is this:
adduction or abduction leads both arms
outward. In the basement, it was for defense.

Out in the basement, the best defense
against grime & smudge is a homemade lemon juice
cleaner. Citrus acid yellowing the cracks of tiles.

Clean citric acid. Yellow. Cracks in the tiles.
A floor not dried. Properties lingering.
My boy body—a dry sponge, waiting for a solution.

Embody a dry sponge. Wait for the absolution
to purify the floor. Soak up hydrogen peroxide tinge.
There is the floor, my cousin: dust.

AMERICAN LỤC BÁT FOR PEELING EGGS

When you are six or eight,
come in the kitchen, take the spot
to the left of the pots—
still warm from those eggs: bought, boiled
& cooled.

Love, you are old
enough now to unfold the skin
back on these white shells.

Love, your little fingers
dig gently. Observe the cracks
you create on the backs
of these eggs.

Love, two light bounces are
all you need to offer the skin.

Coax the fatigued & water it
under the steel faucet.

My child, my love, a
little water can save you from
tiny shards in your thumb.

BUNK BED

The first time I heard what sex sounded like [besides my parents, at night, when I would tiptoe downstairs to sneak out a piece of toast with butter & sugar] was when I visited my brother during his freshman year of college. My brother, who didn't call himself a player but said he just had crushes on girls a lot, wanted me to have the true college experience & had me sleep in his apartment in West Campus during rush week. While he was in the living room, being beautiful & sinking the last cup on the ping pong table, my eight-year-old self was staring at the bottom of the top bunk: its plastic blue stained with something yellow, the springs corroded, the mattress tag ripped in two. The springs began to oscillate towards me, heavy breathing threaded the dusty comforter hanging off the sides. Two lovers, who won't see each other again, lectured me on lust & silence. On observation & stillness. How to be under heat & not be afraid when the tension comes closer & closer towards you.

The first time tension became too close: it was hot & I was afraid. She told me to be still & to just observe. She lectured me, saying, *I could rape you if I wanted to, you know*, my legs dangling off of the bottom bunk. My breath oscillating between heavy & spring. It was in a dorm room during a poetry festival; the mattress was old, ripped in two. My yellow, thirteen-year-old self staring at the springs above, how I envied the emptiness of the bunk up high. Her teammates in the other room, being beautiful & yelling through the door *to get some*. Her teammates wanted us to have a true experience. Told her to *crush it* like I was a ripe jackfruit. Said *I'm teaching you how to have game.* She tried to get my number. Said if I lied, that I would be toast, her nails caramelized into my clavicle, her weight pinning the tips of my toes. The first time I had sex, it wasn't even sex. *It's all oral, baby* she said while I pressed my right thigh against the cold wall—looking to disperse heat. The first time I had oral sex, it sounded nothing like my parents.

TOAST / BUTTER / SUGAR / HAIBUN

Before my father inspected lungs, he worked at a beer factory. *You see this one dent in this twenty-four pack? One dent & it's no good. Guess who gets to bring it home?* His smile, a trophy. These special nights, the cousins & uncles & Tim come over. The cooler thirty-somethings play poker while the more traditional aunts & uncles sing Vietnamese karaoke all night long. My bedroom has no door & is missing half a wall. My room is the game room. My room can't block out any sound. I can't sleep even with all my pillows squeezed against my ears. But my mother, in between love songs & songs about war & songs I couldn't place, comes upstairs to see how I am coping. *You know what you could make us tonight . . .* she says, caressing my face. My eyes widened, excited. *You can even use the white bread!*

The old speaker is barely hanging on. The toaster oven dials down. The top of the body is a light yellow. My mother hits a high note—the words on-screen scroll from white to blue—it is so loud here. The window to apply the butter is getting smaller. My uncle grabs the microphone—he's not reading the room well—chooses a song about two lovers who try to find each other in the midst of war—they don't. My uncle sweats symphonies. The crust on the toast grows dark. I grab the butter from the fridge & with no knife in sight, I smush the fat & protein between my fingers—fingernails turning bronze—open the toaster oven door & wipe my buttered hands over the toast. Like wiping on a towel made of wheat. The butter melts just in time before the song ends. I place each slice of bread on two separate plates: one for me & one for my mother before her next song. She says *be generous with the—*

sprinkled sugar on
top: sweet shine. A special treat
to sparkle the night.

BLESSING THE HOUSE

Come near & kneel
with me on the carpet.
Keep your back perpendicular
to the basement beneath your feet.

Think of your breath
& the breaths that have added
to the air in the living room. The nights
watching movies from Blockbuster together.

Your favorite white sheet
draped over your body by your mother
during the sex scenes. The scenes you could see
through the small tear that you tore on purpose.

Rest your wandering
eye. Allow your memory to become
your mother's hand scratching your back.
The end of the credits where the font is black.

MARIE KONDO IS MY HERO
A LESSON ON FOLDING UNDERGARMENTS

I. ONESIES
fold in half
tuck in sleeves
fold in half
fold in third
fold in third
fold in third

II. BRIEFS
fold the bottom up
fold in half
fold in half again

III. TRUNKS
watch your son
jump up & down
on the bed as you
struggle to yank
the elastic down

IV. BOXER BRIEFS
tease your son
by calling his new bulge
little jalapeño
to see how fiery his face gets;
I wish I could tell you
to polaroid this moment

before he tears up
& yells at you that
he's old enough to
dress & undress
himself

FIRST DAY OF SCHOOL AUBADE

My mother holds my right hand,
her other hand holds a red umbrella

to shield the sun from her eyes. Bright
Houston morning. The condensation

on the crooked stop sign. *Remember*
when you go home to heat up

your cha chien & rice. A secret meal
for my lonesome. I nod & wipe the gunk

from the corner of my eyelid. The bus comes
trudging alone & I clutch the brown

paper bag my mom prepped for me this morning:
ham sandwich [no crust], Hot Cheetos & a can

of Dr. Pepper. I keep the bag crumpled tight
because the inside smells of nước chấm

that my mother accidentally spilled while
prepping my father's lunch. The tall doors

of the bus open & my mother kisses
my cheek. I blush. I let go of her hand.

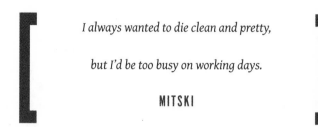

I always wanted to die clean and pretty,

but I'd be too busy on working days.

MITSKI

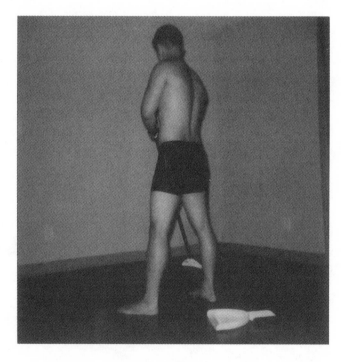

AFTER I WAS MISTAKEN FOR THE STRIPPER WHILE DELIVERING BARBEQUE TO AN ALL-WHITE BACHELORETTE PARTY

I.

If I had a stripper name, it would be *pork loins*. Marinated in my mother's seasoning, I am mostly bone, but my butt is meaty. My neck is long, but you can still love me, if you want to brisket. In the eventual end, it will be my *own* doing. If I had a dollar bill for every human who wanted to see me naked . . . I would still be paying loans back. "Being wanted" was never simmered. I am the lamb's wool & the wolf crying beneath thin skin. Lick between my ribs. Enriched blandness. I am best served with oyster sauce.

II.

& there I stood

a bag of meat

head in the crosshairs

unknown terrain

door closing behind

young deer in the trenches

stay motionless

don't make the first move

kindled fire

feet too warm

apple between the teeth

arrow pointed to the naval

knives & forks

& forks & stomachs

lack of fat

sucked bones

upside down

blood draining

unconsciousness

serpent at my throat

boiling rice

serpent in my throat

not clean

serpent down my throat

III.

Is this what being a sacrifice smells like?

Twenty-six jewel-studded cowboy boots circle me,

tongues glistening in the spur of heat.

DIM SUM DEPRESSION

Watch the gai lan, shriveled,

        drowned in oyster sauce,
legs over the edge of the white plate
        where the white garlic still has some shell,
still wants to fragrant the room.

The shrimp dumpling opens
      before the bite. Cold in the middle,
similar to the touch of the tray
      it sleuths in. Leftover at the end
of the meal. The bill unpaid for.

        Only I like the chicken feet,
           so everyone gazes at the digits
        I cry over. Whip & chew,
           the limbs come alive in my mouth,
        just to fall asleep in my throat.

Bring on all the beef tripe
      from the back of the kitchen. Don't cringe
behind the teapot. Holy cow
      intestines piped by the ginger. Burned
& feared by all who witness.

        Watch the attendants push their carts

into each other. A collision of turnip cakes
who work long hours without a break.
        Paid under the table, pills wrapped
in translucent rice noodle sheets.

SCRATCH MY BACK & I'LL LOVE YOU FOREVER

until your nails break
into my skin. A pedicure
of blood among
the epidermis. Mark
me, your territory, your
dwarf huckleberry. Shovel
into my shoulder blade, unearth
a buried dog-shed of knots—
collar still attached to the chain,
the chain—wrapped around
its post—the post in drool.

AN ARGUMENT ABOUT BEING NEEDY WHILE UNDERNEATH BINARY STARS

A duplex after Jericho Brown

I am afraid of being a light-year
because I fear what lies in the dark.

I fear the dark, because it can be so easy to lie.
For instance: when I said I needed some space,

I hoped you would've read the space
between my breath as a cry for more attention.

You lose air when I cry for more attention,
having to gravitate toward spectroscopic closeness.

Spectroscopic binaries mean our gravities are too close
to the point of wobble. My weight stretched to bits.

There is no point if not to wait for your orbit.
I am nothing at a close distance.

I am close to nothing near the infrared.
I am afraid of being a light-year away.

MARIE KONDO IS MY HERO

A LESSON ON CLOTHING

no
this does not spark
joy but more so this
is the only shirt i have where the sleeves
are shorter

than the waist   not as long
as my neck trust me   i need as many scarfs
as i can get   except   i can scrap this blue one
smells like 2010   all over again
like los angeles smog   but instead   it can see
through my skin   my skin   can't you see there is
no   spark   it's black
from shorting out   hot wire   touching
carpet without permission
a circuit with   no impedance   i
sweat & sweat
the fork red   & prodding
an outlet with   no surge protector
my white shirt
where did they put my white shirt
the one i wore on the plane from houston
with my youth team
where is my coach   they trusted me
to be without supervision
no   wait
you're older than my older
sister but younger than my older older brother
you're old enough to be a mentor

31

[]

turn it on or else
                    i wish
to wrap the missing white shirt
        the pacsun board shorts
                the gray hollister boxers
                        using the white sheet of the   bunk bed
        the one that splits my mind
                        in half
                                just to have
                                        the top bunk
                                                collapse

[]

& & & 2010 a a again all an angeles are as as as as be be black blue board boxers brother bunk bunk bed but but but can can can't carpet circuit coach collapse did does else enough except fork from from get gray half have have hollister hot houston i i i i i i i impedance in instead is is is it it it's joy just keep like like long los many me me mentor mind missing more my my my my my my my my my my neck need no no no no no not not of old older older older older on on one one one only or out outlet over pacsun permission plane poetry prodding protector put red scarfs scrap see see sheet shirt shirt shirt shirt shorter shorting shorts sister skin skin sleeves smells smog so spark spark splits supervision surge sweat sweat team than than than that that the the the the the the the the the the the the the there they they they this this this through to to to to top touching trust trusted turn using waist where where where white white white white wire wish with with with without without wore wrap you younger youth you're you're

black   brother
blue   coach
gray   mentor
red   protector
white   sister
white   team
white   youth
white

AMERICAN LỤC BÁT FOR ADDING COCONUT WATER

This can be bought or found
in the tree
            in the ground of your
living room. The one your
aunt planted
            years before you were
born. A seed that gave birth
to a legacy worth each bruised
palm from each time you lose
your grip
            & fall to roots or feet,
bare feet, black & treated with sun.
Yes, the tree trunk can move
depending on whoever needs a
fresh coconut in the family.
Bow as it walks steadily
into your kitchen.
                        Free the knife
from your hand & grab tight
around its body. Kite your way
up & shimmy your weight towards
the crown.
            At the highest
point holds the juiciest amount
of furry coconuts. The best
part, of this heartwood quest,
is how, with your left arm holding

the ingredients in
place, you will
        get down.

EXHAUSTION [BUT EVERY TIME LEELA ROSE KISSES A RANDOM ASIAN MAN IN THE STREET, A NEW STANZA BEGINS & THE AMOUNT OF WORDS BETWEEN THE BOXES INCREASE BY ONE]

lips [ ] dry [ ] cracked [ ] cornered [ ] unsure [ ] flustered [ ] unconsented [ ] befuddled [ ]

click start [ ] click play [ ] click bait [ ] unhinged jaw [ ] shaky camera [ ] misplaced fingers [ ] white savior [ ]

someone stop her [ ] someone tell her [ ] not your handshake [ ] not your duty [ ] not your right [ ] for a video [ ] YouTube view counts [ ] public display of [ ]

from a haunted past [ ] trapped in the bunk [ ] stuck under the sheets [ ] trapped down the street [ ]

trapped in the massage parlor [ ] if you'd let me I'd— [ ]not enough time to respond [ ] my tongue is not yours [ ] you should ask every time [ ] you should ask every time [ ] you should ask every time [ ]

you should ask every fucking time [ ] every person who looks like me [ ] does not need your expert validation [ ] every person who looks like me [ ] isn't who we see on tv [ ] instead, we see people like you [ ] in front of people like me [ ]

trying to swallow the breath out of [ ] people whose eyes say *keep your pity* [ ] when I see you running up to [ ] kiss Asian people in the street I [ ] remember every finger from my friend's friend [ ] that pinned my cheek to the ground [ ] that told me to not be scared [ ] who locked the room while my friend [ ] strummed "Split Screen Sadness" to drown out [ ] the one year it snowed in Houston [ ] I stayed inside, watching *Rush Hour 2* [ ] cheered when Jackie got to kiss on screen [ ] learned there are two ways to be wanted [ ] one being the pleasant calm you hoped for [ ] the other: where all your will is taken [ ]

tucked between dimples dug deep from not reacting fast [ ] enough, you will not impose your saliva upon my [ ] enough, your good intentions will not make myself masculine [ ]

enough, you have no right to this body, this pain [ ] is not yours to suck, swallow, grope, damage, or burn [ ] my burdens don't need your unsolicited healing, say no more [ ] about how my struggle causes you drowning & just listen

SELF-PORTRAIT AS THE HAND TOWEL WHICH HANGS ABOVE THE TOILET

Yes, the easy joke is that I am *hanging* out
      like I have nothing better to do than dry
            like your hands after you're done with me
                  like no one asks me if it's okay to use me.

No, I do not open my mouth
      wide when the toilet gets flushed.
            Why do you think the horrible of me? None
                  the wiser, when I explain I rest out of "the flush zone."

No, it was not my choice
      to do this type of towel work,
            to do this thankless duty,
                  to do what no one else will do.

Yes, I gaze at the most vulnerable:
      the backs of long, strained necks,
            the backs of skulls that haven't been held,
                  the backs of ears that never listen to my advice.

No, there is more work to be done beyond
      washing your hands. No one asks me to
            watch out for germs, but I soak them all up.
                  Wash the dirt from beneath nails that don't wave back.

Yes, I am lonely,
        I am sad & feel unloved.
                I am sick of the smells.
                        I am wanting a life in the kitchen.

No, not the ones on reality TV, I just want
        the silver of fluorescent across my view,
                the temptation of the oven's handle—sleek,
                        the wild nights of spaghetti & marinara messy.

IN THE BATHROOM AFTER EATING FLAMING HOT CHEETOS

I stand from my porcelain throne   feet planted on tile
gaze into the mirror   say:

                you are the creator   you control your heaven   you prepare
                your hell   you choose   choose again   again you
choose   to continue
                to burn   your insides   your heart
                heartburn   heartburn   hear
        self-worth   burn   the crackle   of your stubborn spleen
                of small intestines twisted   perished pretzel
        drenched   in self   hatred   toxic
masculinity   insecurities   masked as microbes   cleanse by trial-by-fire

        purify   by   boiling
take one hot step   on coal   one day at a time
                & do not fret   hot-head   there is still time to set
                your whole self on fire   after all   you are still alive & that
is praise enough
                & that   is flaming hot

39

COME CLEAN

I lied, I said Wisconsin, but it was a much colder place, let's say Washington.
Truth be told, it was next to a river, that led to a dam, that led to a wash.

I said I blame my cousin, but in fact,
I blame myself. I said I blame the basement, but I blame the washer

that ruined the sound of doing laundry. The violent tumbling
of my body down the stairs, a wet ball of clothing—a washer

falling from the wall, through the drain & out the sink
in Chicago where I am thirteen, laying bare on an unwashed

dorm room comforter, stuck between a bunk bed
& a twenty-year-old body. The roaring wash

of applause from her friends cheering her on. A container too hot,
the pinewood of me melting inwards, the garlic of her breath washing

my innocence with too much bleach. Too much white
on the sheets. Like a massage table, like watching

the ground as the masseuse reaches for the extra tip
to feed their family. How my body walked out washed

in a white robe, my boy mouth telling my uncle
the dirty thing that happened to me as he continues to watch

the áo *dàis* on the street in Vietnam. Says *relax, we're on*
vacation, you're a man now, our happy ending money washed

& laundered. When I get back home, I fold all my laundry
into neat pillars on my bed. I place my body into the washer,

I am a spin cycle of a fetus, playing a game of hide-and-crease;
I win when my stained teeth are all that's left to wash.

I FALL IN LOVE WITH THE SCIENTIST BEHIND THE MASK

Phagocytosis of both our mouths.

New lingerie of loose lips.

Breakfast in a bed of atoms.

Cuddling codons.

Retrosynthesis: the drunken stupor that made us arrive.

Mutation of many many miracles.

RNA wrapped within the legs of golgis.

Exotification of excrements.

Am I the right isotope?

Half-life of an anal bead.

Dilution of idiomatic isolations.

Where are all the electrons? Inside.

SPEAK QUOTIDIAN TO ME

A person who wears shoes in bed will most likely make you cry.

Eggs in the morning get cold by the whisky.

It's good luck if you cut your big toenail & it flings into your eye.

A sugar packet under the table leg makes only a small mess.

Never ball your socks after you've finished in them.

In every immigrant household, there is a drawer of unused grocery bags.

The living room is used for karaoke; the dining room for poker.

A chili pepper a day keeps his temper at bay.

Keep the fish sauce by the first-aid kit.

Threesomes are only allowed in the kitchen with permission from Táo Quân.

If you use your dishwasher for its actual purpose, I don't trust you.

For warding away mosquitos over your bed, a dangling dryer sheet works better than a dream catcher.

Washboard abs are impractical.

Shoelaces tied thrice before bed ensures high fertility.

It's bad luck to stick your chopsticks vertically in your rice.

Chips from the dollar store have their own flavors.

Pack underwear for a trip like you're going to have diarrhea everyday.

Remember you are dust & on dust you shall have bad first sex.

The amount of empty cognac bottles in the house determines how many ghosts return your calls.

ONE NIGHT WITHSTAND

Yes, we can go back to my place. Yes, let's be old fashioned, let's take a cab. Yes, this is where I live. Yes, I live alone. Yes, you can come inside, sorry, my place is a mess. No, no, you're being too kind, my place is usually more spotless than this. Yes, can you take off your shoes if you don't mind? Yes, feel free to have a drink, help yourself! No, sorry, do you mind using a coaster? Yes, I'm one of those coaster-type people. Yes, that's a picture of my parents. Yes, I can put on some slow jams. No, Alexa, John Legend not John Lennon. Yes, now, where were we? No, I do like dirty talking. Yes, you can take off my henley. No, well, hold on, you threw it too close to the trashcan. Yes, well, I don't like the idea of my clothes as trash. Yes, sorry, I'm almost done folding my shirt. No, I don't think we're moving too fast. Yes, we can kiss against the wall. Yes, we can foreplay on the—well, let me put a dirty sheet over the bed. No, it's not like a *dirty* dirty sheet, like a sheet for sex, a sex sheet some would say, but it's like a sheet I put over the bed for when I'm dirty. Yes, exactly, so my dirtiness doesn't contaminate my clean sheets. No, you're right, I'm ruining the mood. Yes, I want you to ruin me. No, you can grab my neck. No, I'm totally fine with it, as long as you washed your hands. Yes, I'm just joking—yes, I know you went to the bathroom at the restaurant. No, I'm not implying you didn't wash your hands, although you technically did touch like three doors on the way here. No, I'm just saying we touched a lot of things today.

Yes, I'll be right there.
Yes, we can talk in the morning.
No, I have to shower first.

FUNNY

as fuck is different than funny fuck.
The dust on the window
creates a funny fuck of a silhouette
byways of sunlight from beyond
the trash compactor.
I, sometimes, watch—well, more
than sometimes—folks drive
their cars with tied-up
trash bags on their roof
like a Christmas tree.
I observe muscled men
attempt to heave greasy plastic bags
over the railing into the trash
compactor. I witness muscled
women swing their arm
as a pendulum & measure
the centripetal force needed
to not walk up the distant,
out-of-the-way, staircase to safely
toss their trash in the compactor.
I've watched grown folks throw
& throw & throw & throw &
fail. I've watched racoons eat
the trash spilling on the floor
below the mouth of the trash compactor.
Full fuzzy bellies having a feast.
Once, I tried walking up to said
misthrown trash bags in order

to place them in the compactor myself,
but then the racoon clawed me
for trying to steal its children's dinner.
Its paws on my neck, saying
you thought, you funny fuck.

AMERICAN LỤC BÁT FOR ADDING PEPPER TO TASTE THE DARK

Be smoke stuck between your teeth
like French-kissing a wreath made of
your favorite colonizers.

Grind into fine sprinkles,
ash like a sprained ankle. Black stone
reflecting a new zone

in the galaxy. Home, in space,
filled with dark matter. Taste of salt
only comes from the stars.

But stars are finicky. Are you
into bright or are you into
infinite? Come to

the dark side. Be the muse
that gets stuck between loose white
teeth, a save-for-later treat.

20 THINGS TO DO BEFORE YOU LEAVE YOUR RESTAURANT JOB

1. Leave your shoes hidden in the back of the walk-in freezer.
2. Trade the locations of the potatoes & tomatoes.
3. Disinfect all surfaces but leave all the handles untouched.
4. Order twenty different things on separate tickets under your employee discount.
5. Spread gossip about the line-cook & the sous-chef.
6. Switch the oven fan from low-fan to high-fan before the brownies go inside.
7. Don't fully plastic-wrap the open avocados.
8. Throw a water bottle in the deep fryer.
9. Tape the front-door key to the ceiling.
10. +1 to every written date on all the containers.
11. Drip mushrooms & onions into the six-pan of spinach.
12. Crack eggs directly into the grease trap.
13. Complete the word search on all the kids menus in permanent marker.
14. Throw a Tide pod into the dishwasher.
15. Place the sheets of bacon in the oven but don't set a timer.
16. Yell to each customer, "WELCOME, NO SUBSTITUTIONS!," as they walk in the door.
17. Use two bottom buns for each burger, bring the other halves home.
18. Label all the white things "cottage cheese."
19. Loosen the tops of all the salt shakers & pepper grinders.
20. Go back to where you left your shoes & place shrimp inside of them.

GOOGLE CALENDAR FOR MY IMPOSTER SYNDROME

GMT-06 · 8 AM – 10 PM

SUN 20

- **Rent Due, 8am**
- **Work Brunch** — 9am – 3pm / How Many Burn Marks On My Forearm Will It Take For Me To Prove To My Father That I Am A Struggling Artist? // How Many White Mothers Will Send Their Food Back To The Kitchen So That I Have Something To Eat? // What Kind Of Sweat May Be Romanticized, Collected, & Studied?
- **Shower (cry)** — 3 – 4pm
- **Touch Yourself Gently**
- **Play Mitski** — 4:15 – 7pm / Because Dreaming Cost Money, My Dear
- **Eat Leftovers From Brunch Naked On The Floor Drinking The** — 7 – 9pm
- **Shower (again)** — 9 – 10pm

MON 21

- **Workout: Push** — 8 – 9am
- **Marinate Meat, 9.30am**
- **Meal-prep Yogurt** — 10 – 11am
- **Talk With Mom** — 11am – 12pm
- **Eat Leftover Laundry** — 12 – 1pm | 12 – 1pm
- **Read Articles For Class** — 1 – 6pm / Comment // Write Notes In The Margins That I Won't Say In Class // What In The White Privilege Is Going On In Here? // Prepare To Say One Unconfident
- **Intro to Grad Studies** — 6 – 8:15pm / How Not To Sound Stupid Talking About Dead White Men
- **Shower** — 8:15 – 9:15pm
- **Call Mom Back, 9:15pm**

TUE 22

- **Workout: Pull** — 8 – 9am
- **Meal Prep Chicken & Rice & Broccoli** — 9 – 10.30am
- **Re-Schedule Work On Draft With Mom** — 11am – 12pm
- **Eat Chicken** — 12 – 1pm
- **Teach Your Students How To Frame Their** — 1 – 3pm / (I Will Never Convince Myself)
- **Work Evening Shift** — 3:30 – 8pm / No One Talks About How Hard It's To Live In A Nocturne // Tonight, I Am The Body That Bows That Should Not Bend // My Hands Are Too Greasy To Scribble That In My Journal // Bring Trash To The Curb
- **Comments For Other Poets Who Are Better Than Me** — 8 – 10pm

WED 23

- **Workout: Legs** — 8 – 9am
- **Office Hours That You Hope No One Goes To** — 9 – 11am / Gossip With The Succulent
- **Call Best Friend & Don't Let Them See Your Work** / **Eat Chicken** 12 – 1pm
- **Clean Toilet** — 1 – 2pm
- **Poetry Workshop** — 3 – 5:30pm / A Discussion On Why Your Sonnets Aren't Sonnety Enough (feat. The Famous Professor)
- **Go To The Local Bar** — 5:45 – 7:15pm / (Downplay Everything)
- **Eat Yogurt, 7:15pm**
- **Shower** — 7:45 – 9:45pm / Play The 'Psycho' Theme Song For Fun

THU 24

- **Workout: Pull / Car Payment / Car Insurance** — 8 – 9am
- **Work On Draft 7** — 9:30 – 11am / **Pre-order Your Friend's Book That You Won't Read For Another** — 10am – 1:...
- **Eat Chicken** — 11am – 12pm
- **Email Your Class Telling Them That Class Is Cancelled** — 1 – 3pm
- **Thesis Hour** — 3 – ... / **Sweep** / **Vacuum** / **Mop** 4:45 – 5:2... / **Protein Shake** 4 – 5pm / 3:15 – 4:15pm / **Organize Your Organizers** 5:30 – 7pm
- **Submission Party / Eat Yogurt** / **Attempt To Bathe** 7:45 – 9:30pm / Eventually Resort To Showering

FRI 25

- **Listen To Mom's Voicemail** — 8 – 9am
- **Work Morning Shift** — 9am – 3:30pm / The Birds Are Too Damn Loud Here // I Get It, Good Morning To You Too // I Made The Bed In A Rush // I Am Not In The Mood // All My Friends Are Writing Somewhere In The North // In The Snow // Or At A Beach // Sipping Margs While Reading Advanced Copies // The Greasetrap Has My Name In It // Swallower of Swallows
- **Workout: Pull** — 3:30 – 4:45pm
- **Thesis Hours** — 4:15 – 9pm / Or Thinking About Writing // Or Thinking About Thinking About Writing // Or Submitting To Journals That I Hope Won't Respond // Or Getting Accepted And Feeling // Nothing– Is It Pity? // Luck?
- **Shower** — 9 – 10pm

SAT 26

- **Work Double Shift** — 8am – 10pm / I Am An Over-Hard Egg Trying To Pass As Egg-Whites // My Ears Take In Compliments As Pity // Close Friends Are The Most Biased // They Only Say Nice Things To Me Because They Like Me // Don't Get Me Started On Family // The Grill Becomes Blacker As Service Wears On // The Oil Burns That Taunt My Knuckles Want To Be Pimples // Strangers Who Come Up After Readings // Also Liars // They're Just Trying To Be Polite // They Haven't Seen Me At My Worst // Or My Least Worst // Or The Growth Of My Worst // Or My Bangs // The Justin Bieber Type Bangs // I Was Hiding My Big Forehead Then // Now, I Hide It In My Hands // Pimples In My Palm // I Know They're There // There, There // The Heat Of The Burners Speak // They Tell Me It's Hot // But My Callouses Are Trained // This Isn't Hot // This Is

A FAILED AMERICAN LỤC BÁT RESPONDS

How much of me must be
written before I am just another
bastardized item?
My accents will soon leave
the letters to float away
across another ocean. Find
them in Texas or Mississippi.
Find them under outstretched tongues,
broken down by enzymes,
spit & fast food. A form can
starve to death, you know? If the libraries burn,
who will think of me? How many
queries until I find home?
A Grecian urn devoid of my ashes:
can I burn enough ink for you?
Can I be read from
fathers who don't speak, who find love
in Vietnamese fantasy,
in warriors trying to find their way home?
O monosyllabic birthplace,
can I self-colonize myself,
be the fusion the world doesn't want to see?
It is written, therefore
it exists in the third generation. The father's
father, the father, the author & now me.
In between self-hatred & self-actualization,
I exist, so who will
abandon me first? Who will shun me

beneath the floorboards? You
or myself? The author or the border?
The home broken by war
or the broken home by the bayou? Shake
the soul out of me: yellow secret
blending in with all the carbon. Suckle-slurped, whispered
& incensed by the head-knee mourners. A mother
will not ask what happened. Instead,
she will take the white headband
at my funeral & burn it with incense
until the holy ghost cries shame.

LAST WORDS

An extended cento after Mitski

When they come for my things,
there will be a note left on my pillow:

I was going to live
for all my cotton tees, folded all the same—

like, did you know the Liberty Bell is a replica?
How it proudly shines its crack

quietly.
I inched away,

silently housed in these original walls
until I became beneath the primer.

They'll never know how I stared at the dark in the room,
but I watched my made bed every single morning

that I couldn't have changed.
No matter how smattered my insides,

I am relieved that I left my room tidy—
one less ugly sight.

I always wanted to die clean & pretty
while my dreams made music in the night.

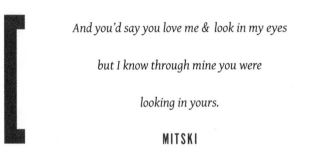

And you'd say you love me & look in my eyes

but I know through mine you were

looking in yours.

MITSKI

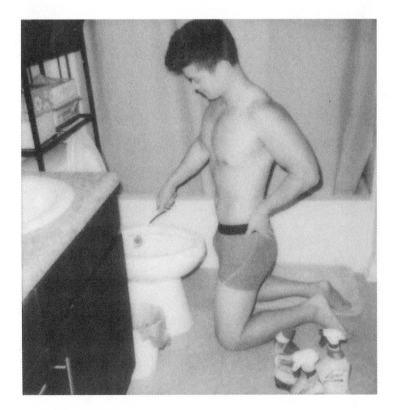

THE RITUAL OF MOURNING HAS CHANGED

At my grave,
bring a warm bowl
of white rice & stick
chopsticks straight up in the middle.
Light the tips
of each chopstick
& bow until your lips
kiss the door
of my coffin
four feet beneath the ground.
Stunned, by love,
chapstick & cigarette breath: a splinter
down the middle
of soiled wood. Crawling, comes
a lotus of dawn, disheveled
by worms, tarnished
by slipped sewage. It slithers
up the chopsticks
towards blue oxygen. Past
the empty bowl,
it dives its head
in a nearby delta
to close again,
underwater.

VIETNAMESE BEDWETTING STORIES IN A DOUBLE HAIBUN

once [ ] I made a mess of myself [ ] turned the white Power Ranger [ ] yellow [ ] fifth pair of underwear [ ] ruined [ ] stood in front of a fan for half the day [ ] to dry [ ] thought about telling my father the truth [ ] instead [ ] thought about sticking my fingers through the metal cracks [ ] either way [ ] he would see red [ ] blood from his belt [ ] below the pantry door [ ] why wouldn't he be angry [ ] working long nights at the hospital [ ] to come home & see [ ] just another accident [ ] a wasted piece of fabric [ ] untimely rip [ ] spoiling soil [ ] untapped potential [ ] I can see the piece of wall my father elbowed [ ] I can still see the carpet where my knees left table marks [ ] *never cry with company over* [ ] so much fluid [ ] so much body [ ]

[the house is soaked]
[urine or tears]
[another accident]

once [ ] my father grew up in Saigon [ ] there was no middle class [ ] just rich [ ] or bones along the road [ ] waiting to be buried in broth [ ] to feed their young [ ] to a soldier [ ] so much racket [ ] was hard enough to sleep [ ] three of his seven siblings [ ] my father [ ] his mother [ ] in one bed [ ] my father woke up humid [ ] crying in his urine [ ] his mother awoke [ ] & without hesitation [ ] without waking his brothers [ ] picked up my father [ ] like the spaces left on the boat [ ] or that family the bay swept [ ] either way [ ] they switched spots [ ] my father watched his mother [ ] fall asleep [ ] without complaining [ ] her heavy forearm a sponge [ ] her hygiene a small sacrifice [ ] puddle of guilt [ ] *that's what love is* [ ] wet & unclear [ ] *orange agent* stains [ ] getting used to the odor [ ] imperfect smeared horizon [ ]

[*cry yourself to sleep*]
[the sheets are the West Lake]
[never wet the bed again]

THỊT KHO

Miles away, I forget to peel the eggs
the night before.

Miles away, I forget to buy the special
brand of coconut juice.

Miles away, my mother is laughing
once I swallow my pride & call.

It'll never be quite the same, she says,
just try your best & finish your food.

When you buy fish sauce,
you must remember to wrap it in newspaper.

If the bottle breaks in the car,
the stench will haunt you long after the car is compacted.

She tells me that it's okay to cry
because the yolks still aren't hard enough.

I am blessed to have a mother who
talks about death, who knows her mortality.

I imagine my mother's passing.
I know she won't have enough grandchildren.

I will have added too much pepper,
not enough boiled eggs.

It's called simmering for a reason:
the house smells of coconut.

Braised pork & hot rice:
rice cleaned thoroughly.

Between the sounds of the blue flame
lies an emulsified telephone cord.

Our recipes will never be quite the same,
but we both wear gloves to peel eggs.

When I cook for my mother,
I know she will lie.

IN PRAISE OF MY THREADED EYEBROWS

After Aimee Nezhukumatathil's "In Praise of My Manicure"

In praise of thread: doubled & twisted. A helix love
        affair between beauty & pain. Tension of pulled
skin. Friction in the form of heat. Praise
        the two hands which grasp my hair's execution.

Not far behind beauty is pain. The tension of pulling
        rows of caterpillar legs from the dirt,
using the hands of gravity's air to perfect execution:
        the monarch leaving its chrysalis behind.

Farewell! Caterpillars resting below the acne
        of my forehead. Hello! Shiny sleek queens
arched with a crown full of crystals. Behind the throne:
        a curtain made of nylon. Yanked apart

across my forehead. I fall in love with the yellow sleek queen
        trimming the hedge above my nose.
Curtailing made from neon. Yank a part of my body
        on the edge of the salon. Stretched,

trimmed & hedged & before I know it—
        there are parts of me that see again.
The edge of the salon outstretches its arms:
        doubled, twisted—helix love of praise & thread.

AMERICAN LỤC BÁT FOR DICING GARLIC

Cut garlic into sixths
or eights—*just put it in everything.*
Garlic in an infinite
loop. Chopped, diced in a skillet. Smash
the blade flat against
a clove. See what senses bring out
the home in you. The mouth
will salivate. Let out a drool.

You're the sticky puddle
right below your ankles. You're
the front door of your far
away house. The friar with a stake
in the vampire. Cut
the garlic to stay put, to stay
alive & healthy &
plump full of hot candy: yellow
& smothered all below the meat,
tucked between the rice. Heat
of the oil retreating in
the cracked cloves.

Let your fingers be wet
& sticky. Your nail beds beige
to the point of malaise.

MY FATHER EXPLAINS EMPLOYMENT

If you ever find yourself
stuck inside a hungry hive,

stick with the drones for the time being,
they won't needle you too hard.

Go find Tony,
tell him that Nhut sent you.

Bring a pack of pilsner
& they'll let you enter

their fantasy football league.
Tony will teach that your place

lies under the queen.

At the end of the summer,
or when the going gets tough,

y'all might get kicked out.
This is the risk of applying to a job you weren't qualified for.

But at least you learn to respect warmth.
& when you are out with Tony, lost

in the meadows without food,
without shelter & without smoke,

then you can come home.

MY MOTHER EXPLAINS UNIVERSAL HEALTHCARE

The bird gives a feather to the sky, like all the other birds do.

The bird doesn't get angry about giving a feather; the bird has many feathers to pluck.

From afar, it still looks like a bird.

One feather a month is for the health of all birds:
blue jays, cardinals, pigeons, hummingbirds, penguins & flamingos.

When a bird hops on one leg,
someone will nurse it back to health
& the bird doesn't pay a feather.

The bird flies on because it should, because it deserves a chance to live.

The bird flows gorgeous with the wind; the wind reveals spots where the bird plucked itself.

You are not a bird,
you are not allowed to fly.

MY CAT DOESN'T GRASP OBJECT PERMANENCE

When the room is ever empty,
that means you are dead.

If you are dead, who will give me
discarded boxes, whose books
will I brush my face upon
until you get all worked up & yell
this is my reading time!

When the shower curtain divides us,
that means you've drowned & I will be left to lick the bathwater.

You go to work & I sleep
for twenty hours in hopes that you wake me earlier
with the sound of the stuck jiggle of your key
& the cave of your forearms.

I know what the temperature of your hands means.

Too cold means to turn on the oven
& make biscuits.

Too hot & I know you just had them inside
your underwear.

Too around my neck & I know
my nails need to be cut so I claw,

I claw into you. Not your face, no, I know
that you need to match your author photo

so you can feed the both of us. I make your forearms bleed,
just a little, just in case you leave for work

& get mauled by a boar. Just in case
you close the bedroom door, the carpet catches
on fire & the window is impenetrable. I just want

to make sure that if this is my final sight of you,
that part of me bleeds into your blood,
so you don't have to die alone.

MARIE KONDO IS MY HERO
ON ORGANIZING CHRISTMAS

a pear tree	dead attic— a worm	pig secret	our snow	ring red glass below finger	company
my wet fat	father's old cross	100 microphone	body & blood	snow	vietnam doorbell

my true love a pear tree fantastic	two dead in the attic— a worm	the pig i learned secret	i can recall four snowballs	ring red glass below the tv screen	company father finger

my wet
 	
my sweet
    fat
	angel i
	
	crucifixed
	on my father's
	old cross
		100
		
		microphone
		
		special
			the homily
			
			body
			& blood
				snow
				
				holiday card
					vietnam
					  my
					brother is
					
					doorbell
					
					break

my true love gifted me a brand-new relationship status under the brown pear tree fantastic wrapping nevertheless	two dead doves at the base of boxes found beneath the fog in the attic—a worm still fresh between beaks	my mother is in charge of cooking the pig every year this year i learned her secret after dropping the pan	i can recall four times it snowed in houston *hey yellow!* snowballs thrown from a bus—also yellow	baby-sized Hakeem jersey fake '94 champion-ship ring red glass below the tv screen	i cried with company over & it felt like my father hit me with his non-eating hand it felt like he hit with an ex-tra finger
my wet dog sweet pup anti-social slept in until spring rolls started cook-ing o my sweet my sweet fat lazy beagle	instead of an angel i placed a chick-fil-a cow cruci-fixed on my father's old cross to fit his catholic values	all 100 sea-sons of *paris by night* the puffy microphone used for viet karaoke on special occa-sions	come in during the homily come in only for body & blood come late leave early avoid eye contact with priest	air is still humid no snow this year break out your best tank-top or go nude for the holiday card	vietnam korea my brother is everywhere but in de-cember the doorbell is just another hi-hat heart break

ODE TO MY BROTHER'S V-NECK

A vertex passed down
from one generation to the next.

      A singular point
      where two brothers meet from across two countries.

            He says he has gained weight
            so it is my job to fill the rest of the fabric.

                  Hand-me-down
                  I use the most: that I hope people ask about so I can brag.

                        Black breathable mesh:
                        a sharp angle to let my chest escape,

                              to let my two nipples peek
                              over the ledge when the air is thick

                        like in Vietnam or Houston or Busan
                        or wherever my brother may be.

                  If I write him enough times
                  he will meet me at the airport.

            Two runaways
            elevating off the ground into an orange sun.

MY SISTER LISTENS TO RUN RIVER NORTH FOR THE FIRST TIME

My sister & I normally do not ride in the same car.
    She is comfortable in our silence.

        [My playlist of Run River North plays at half volume.]

I tell her that John, the drummer, is leaving the band.
    Some people are meant to leave, she says. They have no alternative. Our grandmother
    left us. Y'all weren't as close, but she is to me what I am to you. There is a time where
    your heroes must embark on their own journey to the sky. If you—forever—watch
    how high smoke flies, you'll be engulfed by the sun.

        [Home calls me—I do not hear it.]

    You left too, you know. When you came back, I thought it was for good. Alas, you will
    depart as fast as you came. In a few months, you will travel the world on your own,
    which is to say, your premonition to die young & alone may come true, and I will hear
    of the news late.

        [In hell, your breath will always find you!]
        [In hell, your breath will always find you!]

Is it okay to have doubts in people?
    Brother, our differences are present, but we both hold our feet against the window.
    Remember, your room was once mine, peel the paint & you'll see. We both are light
    sleepers. We both don't know why our father ordered us those embarrassing
    uv-ray-protecting transitions on our glasses. We both can't stand to see mother cry.
    I think you, me & our brother follow this idea that we don't need anyone to be happy.
    We can be happy on our own. And knowing this, we still choose to be with someone,

which makes the love we carry more powerful.

So?

[Lie! I'm a liar! I promise!]

Brother, all I know is this. You are the brightest person I know. Every car on this road may crash into each other. Every driver here may sink into their car seat, airbags failing and glass shattering. Every city may not give the answers you need. And every city may murder you in a different bed with a different knife. But all phoenixes return from migration. & all roads lead back home. Whether you are right or wrong or burning, this home will give you shelter to flame without fear of the sand & I will use your ashes to spell out your answers on the driveway.

THIS SEASON IS MY GREENHOUSE

After Jennifer Chang's "Dorothy Wordsworth"

but do not get your vines twisted,
this isn't a pastoral poem.
This is Jules Charles de l'Écluse hustling
his way to make money in Holland

to pay for cows, car payments
& weed. This is Tiberius sucking
on a cucumber for hydration
with a beluga bulge pressed

out of his cheek. This season
is the cucumber I will slurp
& store beneath mica sheets.
This season will be captured

within cucumber houses enclosed
with sexy *Specularia*. This season
will be the pineapple brought
back to Italy in orange-burnt

cases—O Giardini Botanici,
save me from the wretched
seas. This season will not
be spent releasing humid

air through ceiling flaps
or electric exhaust fans.
This season will be spent
on the thumb of history,

of origin & discovery. Of
building up a safe haven
for us to thrive, to prosper
& to cucumber crunch.

AMERICAN LỤC BÁT FOR MARINATION USING FISH SAUCE

When I open the brand
new bottle, the new management
burns down the door: *You can't*
use that here. You have caught the next
door neighbors in a hex
& I see them bear witness through
their nostrils. They're not used
to this tingle, this tooth that wiggles
above their tongues. They fall
& dissolve. In the hall, they shout,
kick, beg for mercy out
to white angels who part the sky
in half for rain to cry
its cleanse onto July—to wash
away the fresh fish sauce
from my lips. Let me hock & spit
vicious tang on my shit
neighbors. I will sip one last
gurgle & break the flask
of Viet potion fast against
the ground, witness
a hole burn the floor in the way
I start to season a
dish & their mouths will flay open.

I DON'T TRUST THE DISHWASHER

I don't trust the dishwasher
like how I don't trust light in the morning.

I don't trust the dishwasher
like how I don't trust movie butter.

I don't trust the dishwasher
like how I don't trust positive reinforcement.

I don't trust
a process that traps.

I don't trust
my delicates in the hands
of what has no hands.

I don't trust
darkness that is too wet.

I don't trust
the last cycle that ran
through, that tore
the white of the walls 'til
what was left was gape.

I don't trust
mouthwash to do
the job that floss does,

no matter how much
the mouth gargles
the mouth gargles

the mouth shakes
the mouth quakes
door open wide:

                              suds spill.
                    Plates quiver back
                              to still. Trauma in the shape of steam.
                    A spa of floating
                                        wrists, reaching out
                                                  toward my neck, my back, my forehead
                                                            & the gum between my
teeth.
            Gurgled soap in my throat: dirty words
                                        illuminated under gaslight.
Foam bursting out of orifices—organic
                                        lavender down my eardrums, hearing threats
                    disguised as pillow talk.
I should be able to stop
                              the dishwasher halfway.
            I shouldn't have to to wait
                                        for it to be finished. Don't scrub
                                                  a nonstick pan past the point of
purity.
                    I was baptized in a bath,
                    swallowed enough sacred oil
                    for the parish. My own
                                        unconsented renewal: a car wash of my body
during another Texas,
            or New York,
            or Mississippi, flooding. My mother
            swaddled me clean enough, [see page 3],
                                        so all I received, from baptism, was a sacrament

of dry skin.

Let me be born again

in the sink. The dish soap up to my breasts,

my cousin's black teeth smiling

behind the disposable camera.

A pillar of bubbles atop my head,

a gag collar around my cheeks—

a green sponge in place of a red ball.

The sink chromed in a basement in Wisconsin [see page 6],

I mean Washington, I mean— [see page 40]

What matters is that there are no basements in Texas [see page 12].

What matters is that I was seven or eight or nine or eleven,

I was undersized. I was cleaned out.

What matters is I was thirteen

in a bunk bed [see page 15]

in Chicago—

I mean San Diego. I was not supervised,

I fell in love with a painter.

We kissed on a window sill until their coach interrupted.

The window of windex:

the streaks—a smile across my face.

What matters is that another person from another team

blacked out the windows.

What matters is that I was thirteen & they were twenty.

My clothes

burning by the fire exit.

My skin:

broken glass by the fire extinguisher.

The bunk bed: a power dynamic between fire & hand sanitizer.

Afterwards, I lay   sprawled,

a rag drenched in alcohol

below a broken bulb.

I lay face down,

        my cheeks squeezed in the cavity of a massage table,

my eyes becoming coins
    with each pressure point.

    Fifty percent.
        Off with the head. What matters
                is that I was just out of middle school.
What matters is I had an uncle.
What matters is I had a cousin, much younger than me,
with me,
    in another room,
           with the same confused expression.
      I understand, now, what begets the climax of muscles & the rush of
blood:

    hunger. The sacrifice of a Vietnamese boy

      to feed another Vietnamese boy.

        What matters is that I flunked Vietnamese school twice.
What can I say?

    What matters is that we walked out as terrified boys but our uncles called us men.
O, born again
    christening. Joshua—loyal soldier of Moses
    [see Red Sea].

      I still can't get their garlic breath out of me. Again,
    I was young,
      they were old enough to know   better.
        There was snow in Houston [see page 35],
there was my best friend in the bathroom, there was
    her older cousin holding down my wrists,
    there was me:

a target [see page 25],

an Asian-flushed bullseye,

a dive bar pool table with a commercial dishwasher in the kitchen.
The shuddering of its silver body against a rack of beer mugs.

What matters is I can't stand the original purpose
of the dishwasher. Its humidity, its carnage.

The irresponsible lack of awareness of its jets.
The way it bends my favorite spoons.

I leave the lid cracked open, to air
out the debris. To allow the past to dry

on its own time. The methodical process
of wash, rinse & place: I cradle every dirty dish in the sink.

I trust my responsibility with myself.
I trust these hands of warm water.

AMERICAN LỤC BÁT FOR MY MOTHER /
ONE DAY I WILL COOK FOR YOU

Please, Mother, I will serve
you. After years of learning your

recipes, of meat cured
in fridges on the floor, waiting

for the day that the sink
will run warm water in over

my shoulders & after
many failed attempts of stirring too

much ground pepper into
the mix, I will follow through

with my ladle & your
broth.

[]

I imagine the day
my children disobey your rules.

How you will scold & pull
them by their ears. How you'll teach them

angry Vietnamese gems
I never picked up. Then, you will

sit them down with you until
they know that some pain will prelude

love. The dinner mood
set to the key of you asking

if I need help but I hamstring
my foot between you & the stove.

HOARDER

We left everything
          so you could have everything.
Now   we have some things & you
                    want us to have nothing?

Your old trophies   relics: proof
you tried
to make us proud.

Our jade at the bottom of a boat
                              capsized by salt.
Our first couch swept
          by a flood they said
                    couldn't happen in a no-flood zone.

Your father & I gathered
          our urns we collected
& tied them to the boat,
& called it an anchor,
& called it grounded,
& called it land-ho,
          home of the free-range farms
                    filled with meat
          we never have to kill
ourselves.

I could have been the wife
          of a general. Could have lived

in decadence
            of fresh crab meat   pre-picked apart,
but my own mother latched
onto an idea
            of independence.

        Clawed
            onto the image of America:
the sponsor,
the savior,
not the safer.

There are pearls in the ground
                    next to my nieces.

            Argon anklets.

        Necklaces touched by napalm.

        Rings with black nail residue.

        There was no space for trinkets
or tombs.

The dead is a permanence
        more fit for forever frills.

Only room for pockets filled
                with dragonflies.

Just dirty forearms & touches
        by soldiers & your grandmother.

You can clear out your childhood
bedroom; I'll still find

                the permanent marker
                        behind the paint.

But you leave our attic
                alone: a mouth, a stomach.
Cardboard boxes of papercuts
                & newspapered porcelain.

You leave our attic
as is or else I'll tear
                open your belly button,
store my gray hairs in there,
along with your father's fishing pole, & of course,
our tongues.

I'll open you up,
                I'll use a dragonfly as a key.

ACKNOWLEDGMENTS

and gratitude is made to the editors of the following journals in which some of these poems [or earlier versions of them] originally appeared:

Crab Orchard Review: "Thịt Kho"

Frontier Poetry: "Hoarder"

Hot Metal Bridge: "American Lục Bát for Washing Rice"

Litter/Write About Now: "In the Bathroom after Eating Hot Cheetos"

Poetry Northwest: "I Fall in Love with the Scientist behind the Mask"

Rambutan Literary: "My Sister Listens to Run River North for the First Time"

The Offing: "American Lục Bát for Adding Coconut Water," "After I Was Mistaken for the Stripper while Delivering Barbecue to an All-White Bachelorette Party" & "In Praise of My Threaded Eyebrows" [also featured on Tracy K Smith's podcast, *The Slowdown*]

Wildness: "An Argument about Being Needy while Underneath Binary Stars" & "Wisconsin Has a Place in My Heart & I Just Want It to Let Go"

The following poems have appeared in my micro-chapbook, "American Lục Bát for My Mother" [Bull City Press]:

"A Failed American Lục Bát Responds"

"American Lục Bát for Adding Coconut Water"

"American Lục Bát for Adding Pepper to Taste the Dark"

"American Lục Bát for Dicing Garlic"

"American Lục Bát for Marination Using Fish Sauce"

"American Lục Bát for My Mother / One Day I Will Cook for You"

"American Lục Bát for Peeling Eggs"

"Thịt Kho"

"Toast / Butter / Sugar / Haibun"

"American Lục Bát for Washing Rice"

[]

To write is an act of gratitude. When I sit down and write, I try to remember that it is not a solitary act, that there is an accumulation of loved ones who are behind me, being a guide at my elbow. It is an impossible task to try and express my gratitude and joy for everyone who has made this book possible—like a poem, this task is ever-changing, revised multiple times, and never quite done.

I have to thank my family. For my parents, Renee & Nick Nguyen, who drove me three times a week to the Houston Public Library [in hour-long traffic!] during my early exploration of writing. I would like to thank my sister, Tatiana Sethna, for supporting me and my endeavors at all costs, for showing me how love can be modeled and structured like a perfectly wrapped present. For my brother, Robbie Nguyen, who always reminds me of the value of a blocked layup, who reminds me that adventure and learning are intertwined.

I would like to thank Elisa Fuhrken for showing me the sunshine that comes from the combination of kindness and ambition, for showing me unwavering support & love even when I feel like I don't deserve it. Thank you for taking and staging the Polaroid pictures.

My life is nothing without the lineage of teachers, mentors, and guiders that I have had the privilege of being under. Every line written is an accumulation of craft & life lessons that I have sponged. I work every day to make y'all proud. Thank you to my first mentors from Houston: Emanuelee "Outspoken" Bean, Deborah "Deep" Mouton, Dulcie "Digh" Veluthukaran, Jeremyah "The Fluent One" Payne, Ahmad "Nyne" Hygh, and Stephanie Rivera. Y'alls' guidance gave me the confidence to write outside the scope of my limits. Special thanks to Shannon Buggs for organizing Meta-Four Houston, an organization that made me realize my love for writing and for my city of Houston. Thank you to Ann-Fisher Wirth, Beth-Ann Fennelly, Catarina Passidomo Townes, Dustin Parsons, Erin Drew, January O'Neil, Kiese Laymon, Melissa Ginsburg, and the rest of my teachers at the University of Mississippi. Thank you to Derrick Harriell for taking a chance on me & my work & curating one of the greatest MFA programs in the nation. And so so so much gratitude and delight to Aimee Nezhukumatathil for guiding my manuscript with detailed care, affection, & love. I am indebted to you and thank you for influencing my newfound love for the nature around me. Thank you to Lupe & Jasminne Mendez for being in my corner and letting me be part of your family [always ecstatic to get phone calls from y'all!]. Thank you to Sam Sax for your hugs and showing me how to take control of the space on the page. Thank you to Zachary Caballero for reminding me of the joys of language & life. Thank you to Charli Bryan, Corbin Evans, & Cynthia Joyce.

Thank you to Yvonne Simmons, my ninth-grade English teacher, who saw the poet in me before I did.

I am blessed to be in a community with a multifaceted multitude of artists, writers, colleagues, influences, and peers who challenge me to be the best I can be. Thank you to Adam Hamze, Adam Mac, Adrienne Novy, Alison Villasana, Alexa Patrick, Amir Safi, Amy Lam, Angela So, April Lim, Arati Warrier, Ariana Brown, Aris Kian Brown, Ashlee Burnett, Aurielle Marie, Ayokunle Falamo, Bernard Ferguson, Caitlin Thornburgh, Cathy Linh Che, Charles Stephens, Chen Chen, Chris Morris, Christopher Diaz, Cydney Edwards, Dan Lau, Danez Smith, Dani Bee, Devin Samuels, Diana Khoi Nguyen, Duy Doan, Ebony Stewart, Elaine Go, Ellie Black, Emily Pittinos, Enrique Garcia Naranjo, Erin Elizabeth Smith, Fran Sanders, Francine J. Harris, Franny Choi, Gabriel Cortez, George Abraham, Greg Carter, Halle Berry Darry, Hallie Beard, Hanif Abdurraqib, Hazem Fahmy, Helene Alchanzar, Hieu Minh Nguyen, Hussain Ahmed, Ilbersalle Fallon, Imani Davis, Ira Sen, Isabella Borgeson, Jackson Neal, Jacob Dodson, Jade Cho, Jasmine Bell, Jayson Smith, Jean Ho, Jennie Frost, Jennifer Chang, Jennifer Key, Jeremy Eugene, Jericho Brown, Jessica Q. Stark, Joan Osato, Jody Chan, Jordan Simpson, Joseph Flores, Kien Lam, K-Ming Chang, Lara Avery, Latoya Faulk, Laurel Chen, Lauren Bullock, Linda Brown, Lydia Abedeen, Maggie Graber, Mah-ro Khan, Mai Nguyen Do, Marci Calabretta Cancio-Bello, Maria Isabelle Carlos, Mason Wray, Matthew Salesses, Miranda Ramírez, Monica Davidson, Nadia Alexis, Nancy Huang, Natasha Huey, Nghiem Tran, Nicholas Nichols, Noah Stetzer, Noor Al-Naji, Ocean Vuong, Patricia Garcia, Patricia Smith, Paul Tran, Phayvanh Luekhamhan, Randy Kim, Rasika Mathur, Robyn Adams, Rooster Martinez, Rosebud Ben-Oni, Ross White, Rukmini Kalamangalem, Ryan McMasters, Sadia Hassan, Sarah Audsley, Sarah O'Neal, Stacey Balkun, Summer Farah, Su A Chae, Susan Nguyen, Sydney Langford, Tamara Coleman, Tanaya Joshi, Thanh Bui, Tianna Bratcher, Tracy K. Smith, Tyriek White, Victoria Prescott, and Will Nu'utupu Giles.

My friends who taught me kindness, generosity, and friendly competition through board games: Andrew Litwin, Carolina Medina, Elise Doan, Emily Gorski, James Rebullida, Janica Mitra, Jennifer Lin, Jessica Nguyen, Loyce Gayo, Marvine Penson, Rachel Cohen-Ford, Ryan Johnson, Sanjai Sabu, Theresa Giap, Thu Ngo, Tony Nguyen, Vivian Delmundo, Zach Ford, and Zal Sethna.

Special shoutout to the following folks who helped me on my first little poetry tour across the coasts: Adam Melchor, Ashley Nuñez, Gabrielle Bates, Kevin Yang, Libia Marqueza Castro, Nicole Tien, Sienna Burnett, Tessie La, Trisha Do, Tyler Jerrels, and Vy Nguyen.

To my favorite roommates: Noel Quiñones & Julian Randall. Your friendship, love, & work ethic in a shared space is something I will forever be indebted for. I am honored to have our tiles cross in the game of the path. To Andy Sia, our official unofficial third roommate!

Thank you to the following organizations and spaces without whom I would not be the writer I am today: Bull City Press, Inprint Houston, Kundiman, Meta-Four Houston, Sundress Academy for the Arts [SAFTA], the University of Mississippi Creative Writing Program, Tin House, Tintero Projects, UT Spitshine, Vermont Studio Center, Winter Tangerine, Write About Now [WAN], Writers in the Schools [WITS], Yalobusha Review, & Youth Speaks.

Thank you to Marie Kondo, Mitski, & Run River North.

Thank you to Casey LaVela, Dennis Lloyd, Ivan Babanovski, Kaitlin Svabek, Jennifer Conn, Julia Knecht, and the University of Wisconsin Press for handling my work with such care and precision. Special shoutout to my editor, Adam Mehring! Without the entire team, this dream would not have come true. & finally, I would like to thank Carmen Giménez Smith for selecting my book for the Felix Pollak Prize in Poetry; thank you for seeing the life in this book.

& thank you, reader.

NOTES

The rules of the *lục bát* are as follows: in alternating lines of six & eight words, the sixth word of the six-word line rhymes with the sixth word of the next line, which consists of eight words; the eighth word of the eight-word line rhymes with the sixth word of the next six-word line; & so on down one long, uninterrupted stanza. There is also a pattern between flat and sharp tones. Typical themes for the lục bát were warrior culture, womanhood, and a hero's journey. Because the Vietnamese language uses mostly monosyllabic words with different diacritics, the patterned beauty of the lục bát form is both sonic & visual.

The *American lục bát* is a form I created based off of the Vietnamese lục bát that follows the rhyming pattern in six-syllable & eight-syllable lines using polysyllabic English words, resulting in an internal rhyme that helps to drive the poem forward. The pattern can start anew after each line break. Of course, these rules may be adhered to as tightly or as loosely as one would like.

The *duplex* is a poetry form invented by Jericho Brown. I borrowed the form for the poem "An Argument about Being Needy while Underneath Binary Stars." The poem "A Dirty Floor in the Key of Elbows" is inspired by the duplex form.

The epigraph in "Save Me, Marie Kondo" and some of the italicized phrases in "My Marie Kondo Manifesto" were inspired by the book *The Life-Changing Magic of Tidying Up* by Marie Kondo.

"Come Clean" is written in the form of a ghazal.

"20 Things to Do before You Leave Your Restaurant Job" was inspired by a conversation with chef Corbin Evans of The Oxford Canteen.

"In Praise of My Threaded Eyebrows" is written in the form of a *pantoum*.

The three section epigraphs, along with "Last Words," use lyrics from the song "Last Words of a Shooting Star" with permission given by Mitski & Alfred Publishing LLC. An *extended cento* is a form I created in which the first line of each couplet is a borrowed line, followed by an original line of poetry. The last couplet comprises two borrowed lines.

WISCONSIN POETRY SERIES

Edited by Ronald Wallace and Sean Bishop

(B) = Winner of the Brittingham Prize in Poetry
(FP) = Winner of the Felix Pollak Prize in Poetry
(4L) = Winner of the Four Lakes Prize in Poetry